ETFS INDEX FUNDS & MUTUAL FUNDS

The Absolute Beginners Guide To
ETFs Index Funds & Mutual Funds

CONTENTS

Title Page
ETF Mastery: The Beginners Guide To Exchange-Traded Funds — 1
Disclaimer — 2
Introduction — 3
Chapter 1: Understanding Exchange-Traded Funds (ETFs) — 6
Chapter 2: The Structure of ETFs — 10
Chapter 3: Comparing ETFs with Mutual Funds and Stocks — 13
Chapter 4: Investing in ETFs — 17
Chapter 5: Strategic Use of ETFs — 21
Chapter 6: Sector and Industry ETFs — 24
Chapter 7: International and Emerging Market ETFs — 28
Chapter 8: Bond ETFs and Commodity ETFs — 32
Chapter 9: Niche and Thematic ETFs — 36
Chapter 10: Advanced Strategies with ETFs — 40

Chapter 11: Regulatory Considerations and Potential Pitfalls	44
Chapter 12: The Future of ETFs	47
Conclusion: Navigating the World of ETFs	50
Appendix: Resources for ETF Investors	52
The Strategy of Dollar Cost Averaging	55
The Magic of Compounding in Investing	59
The Power of the Dividend Snowball Effect	62
Investing Simplified: Understanding Index Funds and Mutual Funds	65
Introduction	66
Chapter 1: The Basics of Investing	68
Chapter 2: Introduction to Mutual Funds	71
Chapter 3: Introduction to Index Funds	75
Chapter 4: Comparing Mutual Funds and Index Funds	79
Chapter 5: Investment Strategy	82
Chapter 6: Practical Aspects of Investing	85
Chapter 7: Navigating Market Trends and Changes	88
Conclusion: Becoming a Savvy Investor	91
Appendix: Investment Glossary	93
Bibliography and References	97
Disclaimer	99

ETF MASTERY: THE BEGINNERS GUIDE TO EXCHANGE-TRADED FUNDS

DISCLAIMER

Disclaimer: The author of this book is not a licensed financial professional and the information contained within is not intended to be taken as financial advice. Investing in stocks and other securities carries a risk of loss. Please consult a licensed financial advisor and conduct your own research before making any investment decisions.

It is also important to consult with a tax professional when dealing with tax implications of investing, especially when it comes to reporting, as tax laws and rules may vary depending on the country or state and the circumstances.

INTRODUCTION

Welcome to "ETF Mastery: The Beginners Guide To Exchange-Traded Funds", a comprehensive guide that aims to help you understand and navigate the world of Exchange-Traded Funds (ETFs). In the ever-evolving financial markets, ETFs have emerged as a pivotal tool for investors, offering a unique blend of features borrowed from mutual funds and individual stocks.

Definition of ETFs

ETFs, or Exchange-Traded Funds, are a type of security that involves a collection of securities—such as stocks—that often track an underlying index. ETFs are traded on exchanges, much like individual stocks, and experience price changes throughout the day as they are bought and sold.

Historical Background of ETFs

The concept of ETFs isn't new. In fact, the inception of the first ETF can be traced back to 1993, when the American Stock Exchange launched the Standard & Poor's Depositary Receipts, known colloquially as "spiders" (ticker symbol: SPY). This

ETF aimed to track the performance of the S&P 500 Index and quickly gained popularity among investors. From there, the world of ETFs expanded rapidly. Today, there are thousands of ETFs globally, tracking various indices, sectors, commodities, and currencies.

Importance of ETFs in Modern Investing

Today, ETFs play an integral role in modern investing due to their versatility and the benefits they offer. They allow investors to gain broad market exposure, diversify their portfolios, and manage risks more efficiently. ETFs also offer increased flexibility with features like intraday trading, access to nearly any asset class, and in some cases, options or short selling.

In this book, we will explore the world of ETFs in detail. Starting with the basics, we will delve into the different types of ETFs, their structure and workings, and how they differ from other investment vehicles like mutual funds and stocks. We will look into the strategic use of ETFs for portfolio diversification and income generation and discuss how they can be leveraged for tax efficiency. We will explore the benefits and risks of various ETF categories, including sector and industry ETFs, international and emerging market ETFs, bond ETFs, and commodity ETFs.

Additionally, we will cover advanced strategies with ETFs, including shorting ETFs and using leveraged and inverse ETFs. The book will also discuss key regulatory considerations and potential pitfalls to be aware of when investing in ETFs. Finally, we will look at future trends and predictions in the ETF space.

Whether you're a beginner investor looking to understand what ETFs are and how they can fit into your portfolio or an experienced investor aiming to leverage ETFs more strategically, this book aims to be your go-to resource. As we navigate through the landscape of ETFs, it is my hope that you will gain the knowledge and confidence to utilize ETFs effectively in your investment journey. Welcome aboard, and let's dive in!

CHAPTER 1: UNDERSTANDING EXCHANGE-TRADED FUNDS (ETFS)

1.1 What are ETFs?

Exchange-Traded Funds, commonly known as ETFs, are investment vehicles that are built to track the performance of a specific index, sector, commodity, or asset. This could range from a broad market index, such as the S&P 500, to specific industry sectors like technology or healthcare, to commodities like gold or oil, to fixed-income instruments, among others.

Much like a mutual fund, an ETF represents a basket of assets, allowing investors to diversify their investments without having to buy each individual security. However, unlike mutual funds, ETFs are traded on an exchange, much like individual stocks, meaning they can be bought and sold throughout the trading day at market prices.

1.2 How Do ETFs Work?

ETFs are created by financial institutions—referred to as sponsors—who choose the asset or index the ETF will track. To create the fund, the sponsor works with an authorized participant (often a large financial institution), who purchases the underlying assets that the ETF will track and then gives those assets to the sponsor. In return, the sponsor gives the authorized participant shares of the ETF, which the authorized participant can then sell on the open market.

The same process works in reverse when the authorized participant wants to remove shares from the market. They buy up ETF shares, return them to the sponsor, and in return, receive the underlying assets, which they can sell or hold as they see fit. This creation and redemption process helps keep the ETF's price in line with the value of its underlying assets.

1.3 Different Types of ETFs

There are various types of ETFs available, allowing investors to target different investment strategies.

- Index ETFs: These ETFs track a specific index like the S&P 500, FTSE 100, or NASDAQ. They are passively managed and aim to mirror the performance of the index.

- Sector and Industry ETFs: These ETFs target specific sectors or industries, such as technology, healthcare, or financial services.

- Bond ETFs: These are ETFs that focus on bonds and other fixed-income investments. They may target different types of bonds like government, corporate, municipal, etc.

- Commodity ETFs: Commodity ETFs are designed to track the price of a commodity, like gold, oil, or agricultural products.

- Currency ETFs: These ETFs are invested in foreign currencies and aim to profit from currency fluctuations.

- International ETFs: These ETFs track non-U.S. markets or global market indexes.

- Inverse ETFs: These ETFs aim to earn gains from stock declines by shorting stocks. An inverse ETF tracks the inverse of a specific index.

- Leveraged ETFs: These ETFs use financial derivatives and debt to amplify the returns of an underlying index.

By understanding the basics of ETFs—what they are, how they work, and the different types available—investors can utilize these financial tools to build diverse portfolios that align with their specific investment goals and risk tolerance.

CHAPTER 2: THE STRUCTURE OF ETFS

In this chapter, we'll delve deeper into the structure of ETFs, shedding light on the underlying mechanisms that allow these investment vehicles to function as they do. The structure of ETFs revolves around the creation and redemption process, which involves the role of an entity known as an Authorized Participant.

2.1 Creation and Redemption Process

ETFs are unique in the way they are created and redeemed. The process involves a few key players: the ETF sponsor (the financial institution that establishes the ETF), the Authorized Participant (usually a large bank or other financial institution), and the investors who buy and sell shares of the ETF on the open market.

Creation Process: When an ETF is first established, the ETF sponsor works with an Authorized

Participant to create the initial batch of ETF shares. The Authorized Participant purchases the basket of securities that the ETF is designed to track and then delivers those securities to the ETF sponsor. In exchange, the ETF sponsor provides the Authorized Participant with shares of the ETF. This batch of ETF shares is commonly referred to as a "creation unit."

Redemption Process: The redemption process works in reverse. If an Authorized Participant wishes to reduce the number of ETF shares in circulation, they can purchase a creation unit's worth of ETF shares on the open market and then deliver those shares to the ETF sponsor. In return, the ETF sponsor provides the Authorized Participant with the corresponding basket of underlying securities.

This creation and redemption process is a fundamental part of how ETFs operate, and it's one of the main mechanisms that helps keep the price of an ETF in line with the value of its underlying assets.

2.2 In-Kind Transactions

An important aspect of the creation and redemption process is that it typically involves "in-kind" transactions. This means that instead of exchanging cash, the Authorized Participant and the ETF sponsor exchange securities for ETF shares and vice versa. These in-kind transactions help to limit the tax implications of buying and selling securities within the ETF, which can be a significant advantage for investors.

2.3 The Role of Authorized Participants

Authorized Participants (APs) play a crucial role in the operation of ETFs. They are the ones who interact directly with the ETF sponsor to create and redeem ETF shares, and they're typically the only entities allowed to do so.

APs help keep an ETF's market price in line with its net asset value (NAV). If an ETF's market price deviates from its NAV, APs can step in and arbitrage the difference, buying or selling shares to realign the market price with the NAV. This is possible because APs have the ability to create or redeem shares of the ETF at the NAV directly with the ETF sponsor. This mechanism ensures that ETFs are fairly priced and that large price discrepancies are rare.

The structure of ETFs, with the creation and redemption process, in-kind transactions, and the role of Authorized Participants, is a unique characteristic of these investment vehicles. It is crucial to understand these mechanisms to appreciate how ETFs maintain their liquidity and alignment with their underlying assets.

In the next chapter, we will compare ETFs with other types of investment vehicles like mutual funds and stocks, discussing their differences, similarities, and the unique advantages they offer to investors.

CHAPTER 3: COMPARING ETFS WITH MUTUAL FUNDS AND STOCKS

To fully understand ETFs, it's helpful to compare them with other common types of investment vehicles, particularly mutual funds and individual stocks. While they share similarities, they also have distinct differences that can influence an investor's decision-making process.

3.1 Key Differences and Similarities

Mutual Funds vs ETFs:

- Pricing: Mutual funds are priced once a day at the end of the trading day, based on their net asset value (NAV). ETFs, however, are priced throughout the day and can be bought and sold like individual stocks.

- Trading: Mutual fund shares are bought and sold directly from the mutual fund company at the NAV price. ETF shares are traded on an exchange and can be bought and sold at market prices.

- Minimum Investment: Many mutual funds require a minimum investment, which can vary from fund to fund. Most ETFs do not have a minimum investment requirement beyond the price of one share.

Stocks vs ETFs:

- Ownership: Buying a stock means buying a piece of ownership in a single company. An ETF, on the other hand, represents ownership in a basket of different securities.

- Risk: Individual stocks typically carry higher risk because their prices can be significantly affected by company-specific news. ETFs, by virtue of their diversified nature, tend to have lower risk as they spread the investment across many different companies.

3.2 Pros and Cons of Each

Mutual Funds:

- Pros: Mutual funds allow for automatic investment and reinvestment of dividends, professional management, and potentially higher returns if the fund is actively managed and performs well.

- Cons: Mutual funds have higher expense ratios on average than ETFs, may carry a minimum investment requirement, and can generate higher capital gains taxes due to the way they are structured.

ETFs:

- Pros: ETFs offer intraday trading, potential tax efficiency, usually lower expense ratios, and no minimum investment requirement. They also provide an easy way to gain diversified exposure to a specific index, sector, or asset class.

- Cons: ETFs may be subject to broker commissions, bid-ask spreads, and potential discrepancies between NAV and market price.

Stocks:

- Pros: Stocks can offer significant returns if the company performs well, allow direct ownership in a specific company, and can provide dividends.

- Cons: Stocks carry company-specific risk, lack inherent diversification, and require more research and monitoring than mutual funds or ETFs.

3.3 Case Studies Comparing ETFs, Mutual Funds, and Stocks

Case Study 1 - Tech Sector Investing: An investor wants exposure to the tech sector. Buying individual tech stocks might be risky due to company-specific volatility. A tech mutual fund might provide diversification but may come with higher fees and less flexibility. A tech ETF could offer broad exposure to the sector, lower fees, and the flexibility to trade throughout the day.

Case Study 2 - Dividend Investing: An investor looking for steady income might consider individual dividend-paying stocks, a dividend mutual fund, or a dividend ETF. The individual stocks might provide high yields but come with company-specific risks. The mutual fund could offer diversification and professional management but might have higher fees. The ETF could provide a diversified set of dividend-paying stocks, typically with lower fees, and the flexibility to trade intraday.

Understanding the differences and similarities between ETFs, mutual funds, and stocks is crucial when making investment decisions. Each has its own set of advantages and drawbacks that can impact your investment goals, risk tolerance, and expected returns. In the next chapter, we will discuss how to invest in ETFs, including how to buy and sell them, understand ETF expenses, and read an ETF

CHAPTER 4: INVESTING IN ETFS

Having understood the basic structure of ETFs and how they compare with other investment vehicles, let's now focus on the practicalities of investing in ETFs. In this chapter, we will guide you through how to buy and sell ETFs, understand ETF expenses, and interpret an ETF prospectus.

4.1 How to Buy and Sell ETFs

ETFs are bought and sold like individual stocks through a brokerage account. You can place different types of orders depending on your needs: market orders, limit orders, stop orders, etc. While the process might vary slightly between different brokers, the basic steps remain the same:

1. Open a brokerage account: Choose a brokerage that offers access to the ETFs you're interested in. Some brokers also offer commission-free trading, which can be beneficial.

2. Fund your account: Transfer funds to your brokerage account from a bank or another financial institution.

3. Choose your ETF: Research and select the ETF you want to invest in. Keep in mind your investment goals, risk tolerance, and the ETF's strategy, expense ratio, and historical performance.

4. Place your order: Decide how many shares you want to buy and choose the type of order. A market order will buy at the current market price, while a limit order allows you to specify the price at which you want to buy.

5. Monitor your investment: Once you've purchased your ETF shares, it's important to monitor your investment regularly and make adjustments as needed.

4.2 Understanding ETF Expenses

One important aspect to consider when investing in ETFs is the expense ratio. This is the annual fee that all funds or ETFs charge their shareholders. It represents the percentage of the fund's assets that go towards running the fund each year. Expense ratios matter because they can eat into your investment returns over time.

Expense ratios for ETFs are generally lower than those for mutual funds, largely due to the fact that most ETFs are passively managed. However, not all

ETFs have low expense ratios, so it's important to compare fees when choosing your investments.

4.3 Interpreting an ETF Prospectus

Before investing in an ETF, it's crucial to read its prospectus. A prospectus is a legal document that provides details about an investment offering for sale to the public. It will typically include the following sections:

- Investment Objective: This section explains what the ETF aims to achieve. It might aim to track a certain index, invest in a certain sector, or follow a specific investment strategy.

- Fee Table: This outlines all the fees associated with the ETF, including the expense ratio and any transaction fees.

- Principal Investment Strategies: Here, the ETF describes how it aims to achieve its objectives. This might include the types of securities it invests in, the index it tracks, and any specific strategies it uses.

- Principal Risks: All investments carry some risk, and this section describes the specific risks associated with this ETF.

- Performance: This section provides a track record of the ETF's past performance. Remember, past performance is not indicative of future results.

Investing in ETFs involves more than just knowing

how to buy or sell them. Understanding the associated costs and how to interpret an ETF prospectus are crucial steps to making informed investment decisions. In the next chapter, we'll explore various strategies for effectively using ETFs in your portfolio.

CHAPTER 5: STRATEGIC USE OF ETFS

Once you understand the basics of ETFs and how to invest in them, the next step is to integrate them into your investment strategy. This chapter will explore various ways ETFs can be strategically used within a portfolio, including for diversification, income generation, hedging, and sector investing.

5.1 Diversification

One of the primary reasons investors use ETFs is for diversification. As ETFs typically hold a broad range of assets, they can provide exposure to various sectors, asset classes, and geographical regions with a single investment. This can help spread risk and potentially enhance returns.

Asset Class Diversification: ETFs allow investors to diversify across various asset classes such as equities, bonds, commodities, real estate, and even cryptocurrencies.

Geographical Diversification: ETFs can also provide exposure to different geographic regions, including developed and emerging markets. This can help investors tap into growth opportunities globally.

Sector Diversification: Sector-specific ETFs allow investors to gain exposure to specific sectors, such as technology, healthcare, or finance.

5.2 Income Generation

Investors looking for regular income can invest in income-focused ETFs. These include:

Dividend ETFs: These ETFs invest in companies that pay regular dividends. They can be a good source of steady income.

Bond ETFs: Bond ETFs invest in various types of bonds that pay regular interest income. They are considered lower risk than equity ETFs.

5.3 Hedging

Certain types of ETFs can be used to hedge portfolio risk. For instance:

Inverse ETFs: These ETFs are designed to perform as the inverse of a particular index or benchmark, increasing in value when the index decreases.

Volatility ETFs: These ETFs track volatility indices and can help protect against market volatility.

5.4 Sector Investing

ETFs can also be used to implement a sector rotation strategy, where you overweight sectors that are expected to outperform and underweight those expected to underperform.

Sector ETFs: These ETFs track specific sectors, like technology, healthcare, or finance. Investing in sector ETFs can allow you to take advantage of growth in specific industries.

5.5 Thematic Investing

Thematic ETFs focus on specific themes or trends, such as clean energy, artificial intelligence, or e-commerce. Investing in thematic ETFs can be a strategic way to gain exposure to emerging trends and technologies.

ETFs offer a versatile tool for portfolio construction, providing opportunities for diversification, income generation, hedging, and strategic sector or thematic investing. Understanding these strategies can help you use ETFs to achieve your specific investment goals. In the next chapter, we'll delve deeper into the specifics of various types of ETFs, including index ETFs, sector ETFs, bond ETFs, commodity ETFs, and more.

CHAPTER 6: SECTOR AND INDUSTRY ETFS

In this chapter, we will delve deeper into sector and industry ETFs, which allow investors to gain exposure to specific areas of the market. These ETFs can be powerful tools for investors looking to implement strategic, tactical, or thematic investing strategies.

6.1 What Are Sector and Industry ETFs

Sector and industry ETFs are funds that track specific sectors or industries within an economy. They provide concentrated exposure to companies within those sectors or industries. These ETFs are often built to track sector-specific or industry-specific indices.

6.2 Key Sectors and Their ETFs

Different sectors respond differently to various economic conditions, and thus, each has unique opportunities and risks. Here are some key sectors and examples of corresponding ETFs:

Technology: Tech ETFs invest in technology companies. They have the potential for high growth but can also be more volatile. Example: Technology Select Sector SPDR Fund (XLK).

Healthcare: Healthcare ETFs focus on companies in the healthcare sector, including pharmaceuticals, biotech, and healthcare providers. Example: Health Care Select Sector SPDR Fund (XLV).

Financials: Financial ETFs invest in banks, insurance companies, and other financial institutions. Example: Financial Select Sector SPDR Fund (XLF).

Consumer Discretionary: These ETFs invest in companies that sell non-essential goods and services, like automobiles, apparel, or entertainment. Example: Consumer Discretionary Select Sector SPDR Fund (XLY).

Consumer Staples: Unlike discretionary ETFs, staples ETFs invest in companies that sell essential goods like food, beverage, or household products. Example: Consumer Staples Select Sector SPDR Fund (XLP).

6.3 Industry-Specific ETFs

Similar to sector ETFs, industry ETFs focus on specific industries within these broader sectors. This can provide even more targeted exposure. Some examples include:

Semiconductors: Within the technology sector, semiconductor ETFs focus specifically on companies that manufacture semiconductors. Example: iShares PHLX Semiconductor ETF (SOXX).

Biotechnology: Within the healthcare sector, biotech ETFs invest in companies involved in the biotechnology industry. Example: iShares Nasdaq Biotechnology ETF (IBB).

Aerospace & Defense: Within the industrials sector, these ETFs focus on companies involved in the production, distribution, and transportation of aircraft and defense equipment. Example: iShares U.S. Aerospace & Defense ETF (ITA).

6.4 Using Sector and Industry ETFs

Investors use sector and industry ETFs for various reasons. They can be used to express a specific view about a sector or industry, to implement a sector rotation strategy, or to hedge against risks in certain sectors. For example, if an investor believes the technology sector will outperform, they might invest in a technology ETF. Conversely, if they want to hedge against potential downturns in the tech sector, they could consider an inverse technology ETF.

6.5 Risks and Considerations

While sector and industry ETFs offer the

potential for targeted exposure and possibly higher returns, they also come with risks. They lack the diversification of broader market ETFs and can be more susceptible to sector- or industry-specific risks. Thus, it's important for investors to thoroughly understand the specific sector or industry before investing.

Sector and industry ETFs offer investors a way to gain focused exposure to specific areas of the market. When used strategically, these tools can enhance portfolio performance. In the next chapter, we will explore bond ETFs, another important category of ETFs that investors can use to diversify and generate income.

CHAPTER 7: INTERNATIONAL AND EMERGING MARKET ETFS

After covering sector and industry ETFs, this chapter will now explore another category of ETFs: International and Emerging Market ETFs. These ETFs provide exposure to markets outside the investor's home country, offering opportunities for diversification and potentially higher returns.

7.1 What Are International and Emerging Market ETFs

International ETFs invest in securities from markets outside of the United States. Within this category, there are:

Developed Market ETFs: These ETFs focus on countries with more mature economies, such as those in Western Europe and Japan.

Emerging Market ETFs: These ETFs invest in countries with economies considered to be in the development stage, such as China, India, and Brazil. These markets often offer high growth potential, but also come with higher risk.

7.2 Importance of International Diversification

International diversification can help spread investment risk as market performance varies from country to country. It also allows investors to take advantage of growth opportunities in different economies around the world.

7.3 Examples of International and Emerging Market ETFs

Here are some examples of ETFs in this category:

Vanguard FTSE Developed Markets ETF (VEA): This ETF tracks an index of stocks from developed markets outside of the U.S.

iShares MSCI EAFE ETF (EFA): This ETF offers exposure to companies in Europe, Australia, Asia, and the Far East.

Vanguard FTSE Emerging Markets ETF (VWO): This ETF tracks an index of stocks from emerging markets.

iShares MSCI Emerging Markets ETF (EEM): This ETF also provides exposure to companies in emerging markets.

7.4 Risks and Considerations

Investing in international and emerging market ETFs does come with unique risks. These can include:

Country or Region-Specific Risk: Political instability, changes in regulatory policies, or economic downturns in a specific country or region can impact investments.

Currency Risk: Changes in exchange rates can affect the value of investments in international ETFs.

Liquidity Risk: Some international or emerging markets may have less trading volume or fewer investment opportunities, which can affect the liquidity of ETFs focused on these markets.

7.5 Using International and Emerging Market ETFs in Your Portfolio

Despite the risks, international and emerging market ETFs can be valuable additions to your portfolio. They can be used to diversify your investment holdings, gain exposure to growth in various regions, and hedge against domestic market downturns.

By investing in international and emerging market ETFs, you get a convenient and efficient way to explore global investment opportunities. Remember, it's important to research each ETF and understand the risks before investing. In the next chapter, we will delve into another type of ETFs: commodity ETFs, which allow you to invest in physical goods or raw materials.

CHAPTER 8: BOND ETFS AND COMMODITY ETFS

After discussing sector, industry, international, and emerging market ETFs, this chapter will cover two additional types of ETFs: Bond ETFs and Commodity ETFs. These asset classes can further diversify a portfolio and provide additional income or hedging opportunities.

8.1 What Are Bond ETFs

Bond ETFs are funds that invest in bonds. They can provide regular income through the interest payments that bonds make, and are generally considered less risky than stocks. Bond ETFs can be categorized based on the types of bonds they hold:

Government Bond ETFs: These ETFs invest in bonds issued by government entities, like U.S. Treasuries.

Corporate Bond ETFs: These ETFs invest in bonds issued by corporations. They generally offer higher yields than government bonds, but with greater risk.

Municipal Bond ETFs: These ETFs invest in bonds issued by state and local governments. They often have tax advantages for investors.

International and Emerging Market Bond ETFs: These ETFs invest in bonds issued by foreign governments or corporations.

8.2 Using Bond ETFs in Your Portfolio

Investors often use bond ETFs to generate income and to add stability to their portfolios. They can also be used as a safe haven during times of stock market volatility.

8.3 What Are Commodity ETFs

Commodity ETFs offer exposure to a wide variety of physical goods or raw materials, including gold, oil, natural gas, and agricultural products. They can be categorized into:

- Single Commodity ETFs: These ETFs track the price of a specific commodity, like gold or oil.
- Commodity Basket ETFs: These ETFs track a group of different commodities.
- Commodity-Focused Stock ETFs: These ETFs

invest in companies involved in commodity industries, like mining or oil exploration companies.

8.4 Using Commodity ETFs in Your Portfolio

Investors often use commodity ETFs for diversification, as commodities can sometimes move in the opposite direction of stocks or bonds. They can also be used to hedge against inflation, as the price of commodities often rise when inflation increases.

8.5 Risks and Considerations

Bond and commodity ETFs, like all investments, come with certain risks. For bond ETFs, interest rate risk and credit risk are the two major concerns. Commodity ETFs can be subject to price volatility due to changes in supply and demand dynamics, regulatory changes, or geopolitical events.

8.6 Examples of Bond and Commodity ETFs

Examples of bond ETFs include:

iShares Core U.S. Aggregate Bond ETF (AGG): A broad bond ETF investing in a mix of U.S. treasury, mortgage-backed, corporate, and municipal bonds.

Vanguard Total Bond Market ETF (BND): A diversified ETF that seeks to track the performance of the U.S. bond market.

Examples of commodity ETFs include:

SPDR Gold Shares (GLD): This ETF tracks the price of gold.

United States Oil Fund (USO): This ETF tracks the price of West Texas Intermediate light, sweet crude oil.

Bond and commodity ETFs offer opportunities for diversification, income, and hedging. Understanding how they work and how to incorporate them into your investment strategy can help you build a well-rounded portfolio. In the next chapter, we'll explore leveraged and inverse ETFs, sophisticated financial instruments that offer the potential for higher returns, but also come with increased risk.

CHAPTER 9: NICHE AND THEMATIC ETFS

After exploring various broad categories of ETFs, this chapter will delve into niche and thematic ETFs. These ETFs focus on specific investment themes or niche markets that may be overlooked in more traditional ETFs. They can provide unique investment opportunities but also come with their own set of challenges and risks.

9.1 What Are Niche and Thematic ETFs

Niche and thematic ETFs target specific themes or trends in the market. They can cover a broad range of industries, sectors, and even cultural trends. Here are a few types:

Industry-focused ETFs: These ETFs focus on specific industries within broader sectors, such as cloud computing within the technology sector or renewable energy within the utilities sector.

Trend-focused ETFs: These ETFs invest in companies that are expected to benefit from certain trends, like the growth of artificial intelligence or the shift towards remote work.

Socially Responsible ETFs: Also known as ESG (Environmental, Social, Governance) ETFs, these funds invest in companies that meet certain ethical and sustainable criteria.

Blockchain and Cryptocurrency ETFs: These ETFs provide exposure to blockchain technology and cryptocurrencies, either by investing directly in these assets or in companies that are heavily involved in these areas.

9.2 Using Niche and Thematic ETFs in Your Portfolio

Investors use niche and thematic ETFs to gain exposure to specific trends or industries they believe will perform well in the future. They can provide potential growth opportunities that are not available in broader ETFs. They can also help diversify a portfolio and potentially hedge against risks in traditional sectors.

9.3 Risks and Considerations

While niche and thematic ETFs offer unique investment opportunities, they also come with higher risks. These risks can include:

Concentration Risk: As these ETFs are often focused on a specific theme or niche, they can be less diversified than broader ETFs.

Market Risk: These ETFs can be more susceptible to changes in market conditions that affect their specific theme or niche.

Liquidity Risk: Some niche and thematic ETFs are relatively new and may have lower trading volumes, which can impact their liquidity.

9.4 Examples of Niche and Thematic ETFs

Here are some examples of niche and thematic ETFs:

ARK Innovation ETF (ARKK): This ETF invests in companies that ARK believes are leading in areas of disruptive innovation like artificial intelligence, robotics, and blockchain technology.

Global X Robotics & Artificial Intelligence ETF (BOTZ): This fund focuses on companies involved in the development and production of robotics and artificial intelligence.

VanEck Vectors Video Gaming and eSports ETF (ESPO): This ETF tracks the performance of companies involved in video game development, esports, and related hardware and software.

iShares ESG Aware MSCI USA ETF (ESGU): This fund is composed of U.S. companies that have been selected and weighted for positive environmental, social, and governance characteristics.

Niche and thematic ETFs offer opportunities to invest in specific trends, sectors, and values that align with an investor's beliefs and predictions for the future. They can add value and diversification to an investment portfolio but should be used as a part of a balanced investment strategy due to their risks. In the next chapter, we'll discuss the operational aspects of investing in ETFs, including how to buy and sell ETFs, tax considerations, and more.

CHAPTER 10: ADVANCED STRATEGIES WITH ETFS

Having covered the different types of ETFs and their uses, this chapter will introduce advanced strategies with ETFs. These strategies can be used to manage risk, enhance returns, and achieve specific investment goals.

10.1 Short Selling ETFs

Short selling involves selling securities that you do not own, with the intention of buying them back later at a lower price. This can be done with ETFs, allowing investors to profit from a decline in the value of the underlying assets. However, short selling carries significant risk, as potential losses are theoretically unlimited.

10.2 Leveraged and Inverse ETFs

Leveraged ETFs seek to deliver multiples of the performance of the index or benchmark they track. They use financial derivatives and debt to amplify the returns of an underlying index.

Inverse ETFs, on the other hand, are designed to profit from a decline in the value of an underlying benchmark. These ETFs also use derivatives to achieve their goals.

Both leveraged and inverse ETFs are complex financial instruments that come with significant risk and are generally suitable for experienced traders and investors.

10.3 ETFs and Options Strategies

Options are financial derivatives that give the holder the right, but not the obligation, to buy or sell an asset at a specific price within a certain period. ETF options can be used to hedge against potential losses, generate income, or speculate on the price movements of the underlying ETF.

10.4 Tax-Efficient Investing with ETFs

ETFs can in some instances be more tax-efficient than mutual funds due to their structure. Strategies such as holding ETFs longer than one year for long-term capital gains, strategically harvesting tax losses, and gifting or donating appreciated ETF shares can help optimize after-tax returns.

10.5 Portfolio Construction and Asset Allocation with ETFs

ETFs can be used in advanced portfolio construction and asset allocation strategies. These can include strategic asset allocation, tactical asset allocation, and core-satellite investing strategies.

10.6 Risks and Considerations

Advanced strategies with ETFs can be complex and come with significant risks. They require a good understanding of financial markets and instruments, and they may not be suitable for all investors. Therefore, it's important to thoroughly understand these strategies, or consult with a financial advisor, before implementing them.

10.7 Examples of ETFs Used in Advanced Strategies

Here are some examples of ETFs used in advanced strategies:

ProShares UltraPro QQQ (TQQQ): This is a leveraged ETF that seeks to deliver three times the daily performance of the NASDAQ-100 Index.

ProShares Short S&P500 (SH): An inverse ETF that aims to deliver the opposite of the daily performance of the S&P 500 Index.

SPDR S&P 500 ETF Trust (SPY): One of the most heavily traded ETFs in the world, SPY has a very active options market.

Advanced strategies with ETFs can help investors achieve specific investment goals, manage risk, and potentially enhance returns. However, these strategies require knowledge and understanding of financial markets and instruments. In the next chapter, we'll discuss the future of ETFs, including new trends and developments in the ETF market.

CHAPTER 11: REGULATORY CONSIDERATIONS AND POTENTIAL PITFALLS

Having traversed through the landscape of various ETFs and their advanced strategies, it's crucial to also understand the regulatory considerations and potential pitfalls associated with investing in ETFs. This chapter discusses these elements in detail.

11.1 Understanding the Regulatory Framework

ETFs are regulated by financial regulatory bodies, such as the Securities and Exchange Commission (SEC) in the United States. They are subject to the Investment Company Act of 1940 and must meet certain requirements in terms of transparency, diversification, and management.

11.2 Important Disclosures

ETFs are required to publish their holdings on a daily basis. This level of transparency allows investors to understand the fund's exact portfolio composition at any given time. Furthermore, ETF prospectuses, which include information about the fund's investment objective, strategies, risks, and costs, should be carefully reviewed before investing.

11.3 Potential Pitfalls and Risks

While ETFs have many benefits, they also come with potential pitfalls:

Market Risk: ETFs are subject to market risk, meaning the price of shares can go up or down in response to the performance of the underlying assets and broader market movements.

Liquidity Risk: While ETFs are generally liquid, certain niche or less popular ETFs might have lower trading volumes, leading to wider bid-ask spreads.

Tracking Error: This is the divergence between the ETF's performance and the performance of the underlying index. Tracking error can be caused by fees, rebalancing, or logistical issues.

Counterparty Risk: This applies mainly to synthetic ETFs, which use derivatives and swaps to track an index. If the counterparty defaults, the ETF could lose money.

11.4 The Risks of Leveraged and Inverse ETFs

Leveraged and inverse ETFs, as covered in previous chapters, carry additional risk. They are generally more suited to experienced investors and are often used for short-term trading rather than long-term investing.

11.5 Tax Considerations

While ETFs are known for their tax efficiency, some ETFs, particularly those investing in commodities or currencies, may have different tax implications. It is important to understand the tax consequences of your investments.

11.6 The Role of a Financial Advisor

Given the complexity and potential pitfalls of ETF investing, many investors seek the help of a financial advisor. An advisor can help to clarify the benefits and risks of different ETFs and can assist in creating a portfolio that aligns with the investor's risk tolerance and goals.

Investing in ETFs, while offering numerous benefits, comes with its own set of regulatory considerations and potential pitfalls. Being aware of these factors can greatly enhance your understanding of this financial instrument and help you make informed decisions. In the final chapter, we will discuss the future of ETFs, focusing on new trends and potential developments in the ETF landscape.

CHAPTER 12: THE FUTURE OF ETFS

As we conclude our journey through the world of Exchange-Traded Funds (ETFs), it is crucial to look forward to the emerging trends and potential future developments in the ETF landscape. This chapter will discuss these themes, providing a glimpse of the future of ETF investing.

12.1 Innovation and New Products

The ETF industry has seen continuous innovation since its inception, with fund providers consistently introducing new products to meet evolving investor needs. This trend is likely to continue, with the development of more niche and thematic ETFs, as well as the potential introduction of ETFs based on new asset classes or investing strategies.

12.2 Growth of ESG ETFs

The rise of Environmental, Social, and Governance (ESG) investing has been one of the biggest trends in the investment world in recent years. As more investors seek to align their investments with their values, the demand for ESG ETFs is expected to increase, leading to the introduction of more ESG-focused funds.

12.3 Regulatory Changes

Changes in regulatory frameworks can significantly impact the ETF industry. Potential future regulatory changes could either create new opportunities for the industry or introduce new challenges. For instance, there has been an ongoing debate around the potential introduction of ETFs that invest in cryptocurrencies, which could open up new investment opportunities if approved by regulatory bodies.

12.4 Technology and ETFs

Technology continues to revolutionize the financial industry, and ETFs are no exception. Advances in financial technology could lead to more efficient trading platforms, better transparency, and more accurate tracking of underlying assets. Furthermore, blockchain technology could potentially disrupt the way ETFs are created and traded.

12.5 Investor Education

As the ETF industry grows and evolves, so too does the need for investor education. Investors need to understand the benefits and risks of ETFs, as well as how to use them effectively in their portfolios. As such, financial literacy and investor education will likely become an increasingly important focus for the industry.

12.6 Potential Risks and Challenges

Despite the many opportunities for growth, the ETF industry also faces potential risks and challenges. These could include market volatility, regulatory changes, or economic downturns that impact investor sentiment. ETF providers will need to navigate these challenges while continuing to provide value to their investors.

In conclusion, the future of ETFs is bright, but not without challenges. The ability to adapt and evolve will be key to the continued success of the ETF industry. By understanding these future trends and developments, investors can make more informed decisions and be better prepared for the future of ETF investing.

CONCLUSION: NAVIGATING THE WORLD OF ETFS

Exchange-Traded Funds (ETFs) have emerged as a powerful tool in the world of investing, providing investors with a versatile means to diversify their portfolios, manage risk, and gain exposure to a broad array of asset classes, sectors, and strategies. They have democratized investing, enabling individual investors to access opportunities that were once exclusive to institutions or very wealthy individuals.

Throughout this book, we've explored the structure of ETFs, compared them with other financial instruments, discussed various types of ETFs, and delved into strategies for investing in them. We've navigated regulatory considerations and potential pitfalls and peeked into the promising future of ETFs.

Despite their many advantages, it's important

to remember that, like any investment, ETFs come with their own set of risks. These risks can be mitigated through careful research, prudent decision-making, and ongoing monitoring of your investments. It's crucial to align your ETF investments with your financial goals, risk tolerance, and investment timeline.

If there's one key takeaway from this book, it's that knowledge is power. The more you understand about ETFs and the way they operate, the better equipped you'll be to leverage their potential benefits while minimizing potential pitfalls.

ETFs are a dynamic, evolving field with innovations and developments continuously emerging. To stay informed and adaptable in this environment, ongoing education is crucial. In this rapidly changing world of investing, it's essential to keep learning, keep questioning, and keep evolving.

As we wrap up our journey through the world of ETFs, remember that the learning doesn't stop here. May this book serve as a guide, a reference point, and a catalyst for further exploration as you continue your investment journey in the exciting world of ETFs.

APPENDIX: RESOURCES FOR ETF INVESTORS

To help you continue your journey in understanding and investing in ETFs, we've compiled a list of resources that can provide further insights and guidance.

A. Websites and Online Resources

ETF.com: A comprehensive resource providing news, analysis, and educational content about ETFs.
Morningstar: Known for its investment research, Morningstar offers robust analysis of ETFs.
Yahoo Finance ETF Center: This platform provides a wide range of information about different ETFs, including performance data, holdings, and news.

B. Financial News Sites

Bloomberg: Covers global financial news and provides in-depth coverage and analysis of ETFs.
Financial Times: Its ETF Hub provides news and

analysis on the latest developments in the ETF world.

Wall Street Journal: Offers a range of financial news, including updates and insights on ETFs.

C. Books

"The ETF Book: All You Need to Know About Exchange-Traded Funds" by Richard A. Ferri: This book offers a comprehensive look at the world of ETFs.

"Exchange-Traded Funds for Dummies" by Russell Wild: A great starting point for beginners to understand ETFs.

"The Little Book of Common Sense Investing" by John C. Bogle: While not exclusively about ETFs, this book by the founder of Vanguard provides valuable insights into index investing.

D. Blogs and Forums

Bogleheads Forum: Named in honor of John Bogle, the Bogleheads community is a treasure trove of knowledge about index investing and ETFs.

Seeking Alpha: This platform provides a wealth of crowd-sourced articles and discussions on ETFs.

Reddit's r/investing: This subreddit often features discussions on ETFs.

E. Regulatory Resources

Securities and Exchange Commission (SEC): The SEC's website provides regulatory news and guidance related to ETFs.

Financial Industry Regulatory Authority (FINRA): FINRA offers a range of investor education resources, including those related to ETFs.

F. Financial Advisors

While not a specific resource, a financial advisor can provide personalized advice on investing in ETFs based on your individual circumstances and goals. When choosing a financial advisor, be sure to consider their qualifications, fees, and whether their approach aligns with your investment philosophy.

Note: This appendix is not exhaustive and the relevance of resources may change over time. It is always beneficial to seek out the most recent and relevant resources as you continue your ETF investment journey.

THE STRATEGY OF DOLLAR COST AVERAGING

Dollar-cost averaging (DCA) is a tried-and-true investment technique designed to reduce the impact of volatility in the purchasing price of your investments. Instead of investing a large sum of money in a single lump sum, you spread your investment out over time, investing smaller amounts regularly. This strategy not only can minimize risk but also instills a discipline that encourages continual investment, regardless of market conditions.

Let's dive in and illustrate how this technique works with a few simple examples.

Example 1: Consistent Purchase Prices

Imagine a world where the price of an investment remains constant over time. Let's say you decide to invest $100 per month in a mutual fund whose price per share remains steady at $10. Every month, your $100 investment buys you 10 shares. Over the course of a year, you've accumulated 120 shares, and you've invested $1,200. In this scenario, your average purchase price per share is $10, the same as the constant market price.

Example 2: Fluctuating Market Conditions

Now let's add some realism to the scenario. Prices in the real market don't stay constant; they fluctuate. Let's consider a scenario where the share price of your chosen mutual fund moves up and down over six months. In January, the price per share is $10. In February, it's $8. In March, it rises to $12. In April, it drops to $9. In May, it climbs to $13, and in June, it falls again to $11.

Despite these fluctuations, you stick to your strategy, investing your steady $100 every month. In January, you purchase 10 shares; in February, 12.5 shares; in March, 8.33 shares; in April, 11.11 shares; in May, 7.69 shares; and in June, 9.09 shares. By the end of June, you have accumulated 58.72 shares, investing a total of $600.

The average market price of the share over these six months was $10.50. However, due to dollar-cost averaging, your average cost per share ends up being around $10.23 ($600 divided by 58.72 shares). Despite the fluctuating market, your regular investment schedule allowed you to buy more shares when the price was low and fewer when the price was high.

Example 3: Market Downtrend

Let's consider a more pessimistic scenario: a declining market. Over six months, the share price drops from $10 in January to $9 in February, $8 in March, $7 in April, $6 in May, and finally to $5 in June.

Again, you stick to your investment schedule, purchasing shares every month with your $100. You end up buying more shares when the prices are low and fewer when the prices are high. By the end of June, despite the falling market, you've accumulated 77.78 shares for a total investment of $600.

The average market price per share during this period was $7.50, while your average cost per share ended up around $7.72. Even in a falling market, your losses were somewhat mitigated because you purchased more shares when prices were low.

These examples illustrate how dollar-cost averaging can help an investor navigate the uncertainties of the market. By investing a fixed amount on a regular schedule, you buy more shares when prices are low and fewer when they're high. Over time, this strategy can result in a lower average cost per share compared to the average market price.

It's important to remember, however, that while dollar-cost averaging can lower the risk of investing a large amount in a single investment at the wrong time, it does not guarantee a profit or protect against loss in declining markets. Always consider your risk tolerance and investment goals before deciding on an investment strategy.

THE MAGIC OF COMPOUNDING IN INVESTING

Compounding, often referred to as the eighth wonder of the world, is a foundational concept in investing. It refers to the process of earning returns not only on the original investment but also on the reinvested earnings, which grow exponentially over time. This chapter will delve into the intricacies of compounding in investing, using illustrative examples.

The magic of compounding becomes evident when you leave your investment and its returns untouched over a long period of time. In this scenario, not only does your initial investment yield returns, but those returns yield further returns themselves, and so on. This chain reaction creates a snowball effect, where your wealth can grow faster and faster as time goes on.

To make it easier to understand, let's use a simple

example and examine it step by step.

Example 1: Understanding Compounding

Suppose you have $10,000 to invest, and you find an investment that offers an annual interest rate of 5%. If you invest your $10,000, at the end of one year, you would earn $500 in interest (5% of $10,000), making your total investment worth $10,500.

If you leave this amount untouched for another year, the interest for the second year would be $525 (5% of $10,500). The interest is higher this year because it's calculated on the new total amount, which includes the interest from the previous year. This is where the magic of compounding starts to become apparent.

Let's see how this investment evolves over 20 years if the interest is compounded annually.

By the end of the 20th year, your initial investment of $10,000 has grown to about $26,533 without you adding any more money. More than half of this amount is the result of interest earned on interest – the magic of compounding.

Example 2: The Power of Time in Compounding

The power of compounding increases with time. To illustrate this, let's add another character to our example, Bob, who also starts with $10,000 but begins investing ten years later than you did. Bob invests his money in the same venture offering an annual interest rate of 5%.

In ten years, Bob's investment grows to $16,289. While it's a respectable sum, when we compare it to your investment, the difference is stark. Your investment, compounded over 20 years, has grown to $26,533 – more than $10,000 higher than Bob's sum, even though the original principal was the same. This example shows the dramatic effect time can have on compound growth.

Compounding is a potent force in investing. The more time your money has to grow, the more profound the compounding effect becomes. The combination of steady returns and time can create impressive outcomes, turning even small but regular investments into significant sums. Remember, the key ingredients for successful compounding are reinvesting your earnings and giving your investment time to grow.

The principle of compounding underpins the wisdom of starting to invest as early as possible and being patient. It's not about making a quick buck, but about letting your money work for you over the long haul. Embrace the magic of compounding, and you could see remarkable growth in your investments.

THE POWER OF THE DIVIDEND SNOWBALL EFFECT

The concept of the "Dividend Snowball" is a metaphorical representation of how the process of reinvesting dividends can lead to significant growth in an investment portfolio over time. Just as a small snowball rolling downhill can become larger as it accumulates more snow, so too can the process of reinvesting dividends lead to the growth of an investment portfolio as it accumulates and reinvests more dividends.

The idea here is simple, yet powerful. When you receive dividends from an investment, instead of taking that money out of your account and spending it, you reinvest it by purchasing more shares of the investment. These new shares, in turn, generate their own dividends, which you can then reinvest again, leading to a compounding effect. Over time, your investments can grow exponentially, all because you chose to let your dividends work for you.

Let's illustrate this concept with an example.

Example: Building a Dividend Snowball

Consider an investor, Alice, who invests $10,000 in a dividend-paying stock. Let's assume that the stock has a dividend yield of 4% and that the price of the stock increases by an average of 5% per year.

In the first year, Alice's investment earns her $400 in dividends (4% of $10,000). If Alice decides to reinvest these dividends by purchasing more shares of the stock, her investment at the end of the year is now worth $10,400.

In the second year, the investment generates $416 in dividends (4% of $10,400), and the total value of the investment grows to $10,816. Notice that the dividends earned in the second year are slightly more than the dividends earned in the first year because of the additional shares purchased with the reinvested dividends.

Let's fast forward to the tenth year. By now, assuming Alice continued to reinvest her dividends each year, her initial $10,000 investment has grown to approximately $14,802, generating about $592 in annual dividends. That's nearly 50% more in dividends per year compared to what the investment was generating in the first year.

And this is where the 'snowball effect' becomes evident. As Alice continues to reinvest the dividends, the rate of growth of her investment accelerates. Twenty years down the line, her initial $10,000 investment would have swelled to about $32,434, providing an annual dividend income of $1,297. That's more than triple the dividends compared to year one!

It's important to note that this example assumes a constant dividend yield and steady growth in the stock price, which is unlikely in the real world. Prices fluctuate and companies can decide to change their dividend policies. However, this simplification helps us understand the basic principle of the dividend snowball effect.

The strategy of reinvesting dividends allows your investment to grow exponentially over the long term. It's a relatively low-effort way to significantly increase your income from investments over time. So, the next time you receive dividends, consider rolling them back into your investment snowball and watch as it grows larger and larger over time.

INVESTING SIMPLIFIED: UNDERSTANDING INDEX FUNDS AND MUTUAL FUNDS

INTRODUCTION

Welcome to "Investing Simplified: Understanding Index Funds and Mutual Funds". Whether you're a novice investor dipping your toes into the world of finance, or an experienced professional looking for a comprehensive overview, this book is designed to guide you through the maze of index funds and mutual funds.

The decision to invest is a significant step towards securing your financial future. Yet, the sheer number of investment options can be overwhelming. This book seeks to simplify two crucial types of investments—index funds and mutual funds, demystifying their workings and showing you how they could form a part of your financial portfolio.

Our goal is to provide a lucid and accessible understanding of these investment vehicles. We'll strip away the jargon, examine the underlying principles, and focus on practical, actionable insights. After reading this book, you will have a clear understanding of the similarities and differences between index funds and mutual funds.

Additionally, you will have a better grasp of how they can play a role in your investment strategy, and be able to make informed decisions about your financial future.

Achieving financial literacy is a long-term process, just like running a marathon. It requires consistent effort and dedication to reach the finish line. It's about arming oneself with knowledge and making informed decisions that align with your financial goals and risk tolerance. As such, this book isn't just about explaining what index funds and mutual funds are. It's about helping you build a solid foundation for your investment journey and empowering you to take control of your financial destiny.

In the chapters that follow, we will delve into the basics of investing before introducing mutual funds and index funds. We'll explore their benefits and drawbacks, compare their features, and discuss how to incorporate them into your investment strategy. Practical aspects of investing such as account opening, fund selection, investment monitoring, and tax considerations will also be covered.

I invite you to approach this book with an open mind and an eagerness to learn. Remember, every investor started at the beginning, and every step you take is a step towards greater financial confidence. Welcome to your journey into the world of index funds and mutual funds. Let's begin.

CHAPTER 1: THE BASICS OF INVESTING

Investing is a critical component of personal finance management. Understanding the basics of investing can help you make well-informed decisions, mitigate potential risks, and maximize your returns. This chapter will guide you through the fundamental concepts of investing and provide a strong foundation for your understanding of index funds and mutual funds.

1.1 What is Investing?

Investing is the process of allocating money or resources with the expectation of generating an income or profit. When you invest, you purchase assets such as stocks, bonds, real estate, or mutual funds, intending to sell them later for a higher price or to generate income over time. The aim is to create wealth over the long term, providing a return that outpaces inflation and increases your purchasing power.

1.2 Different Types of Investments

Investments come in various forms, each with their own risk and reward characteristics. Let me provide you with an overview of the primary forms of investments available.:

- Stocks: Buying shares of a company makes you a part-owner of that business. Stocks have high growth potential but also come with significant risk.

- Bonds: A bond is essentially a loan you give to an entity (like a corporation or government). They promise to pay you back with interest after a certain period.

- Real Estate: This includes investing in properties for rental income or capital appreciation.

- Mutual Funds and Index Funds are investments that gather funds from multiple investors to purchase a varied range of assets.

1.3 Risk and Return

All investments involve a trade-off between risk and return. It is commonly understood that there is a direct correlation between the potential returns and risk involved in any investment. The higher the potential returns, the higher the risk. Your comfort level with this risk-return trade-off, known as your risk tolerance, is a key factor in determining your investment strategy.

1.4 Time Value of Money

The time value of money is a fundamental financial concept that dictates that a dollar today is worth more than a dollar in the future. This principle is the basis for earning interest on your investments and emphasizes the importance of investing early.

In the next chapters, we will focus on mutual funds and index funds, two popular investment vehicles that allow you to pool your money with other investors to purchase a diversified portfolio of assets. By understanding the basics of investing, you are now equipped to delve deeper into these types of investments and make informed decisions about which might be best for you.

CHAPTER 2: INTRODUCTION TO MUTUAL FUNDS

Mutual funds are a key part of many investment portfolios. By pooling resources from numerous investors, these funds offer diversification and professional management that might otherwise be out of reach for individual investors. This chapter will introduce you to the basics of mutual funds, including their history, types, benefits, drawbacks, and how they operate.

2.1 Definition and History of Mutual Funds

A mutual fund is an investment vehicle that collects money from many investors and uses it to buy a diversified portfolio of stocks, bonds, or other assets. Each investor in the fund owns shares, which represent a portion of the holdings of the fund.

The history of mutual funds dates back to the 18th

century in Europe, but they gained popularity in the United States in the 20th century. Today, they are a staple in the portfolios of millions of investors worldwide.

2.2 Types of Mutual Funds

Mutual funds can be classified into several categories based on the type of securities they invest in, investment objective, and risk level:

- Equity Funds: primarily invest in stocks. They can focus on certain sectors, company sizes, or geographical areas.

- Fixed Income Funds: These invest in bonds or other debt securities. Their goal is to offer consistent income to investors.

- Money Market Funds: These funds invest in short-term, high-quality investments and are considered low risk.

- Balanced or Hybrid Funds: These invest in a mix of stocks and bonds to balance growth and income.

2.3 The Benefits of Investing in Mutual Funds

Mutual funds offer several advantages to investors:

- Diversification: Mutual funds can invest in a wide range of securities, reducing the risk associated with any single investment.

- Professional Management: Mutual funds are

managed by professional fund managers who make investment decisions on behalf of the fund's shareholders.

- Accessibility: With low minimum investment requirements, mutual funds are accessible to individual investors who might not be able to build a diversified portfolio on their own.

2.4 The Drawbacks of Investing in Mutual Funds

Despite their benefits, mutual funds also have some drawbacks:

- Costs: Mutual funds charge fees, known as expense ratios, for the management and operation of the fund. Some also charge sales commissions, known as loads.

- Limited Control: Investors in a mutual fund don't have control over the specific securities in the portfolio.

- Potential for Underperformance: Not all mutual funds perform well. Some may fail to meet their objectives, or they may underperform the broader market.

2.5 The Mechanics of Mutual Funds: NAV, Purchase, and Sale

The price per share of a mutual fund is referred to as its net asset value (NAV). It's calculated daily based on the total value of the fund's assets minus its liabilities, divided by the number of shares outstanding.

Investors can buy or sell mutual fund shares directly from the fund (or through a broker) at the current NAV, plus any sales charge. Mutual fund transactions are executed at the next available NAV after the order is received, not the current market price as with stocks.

In the next chapter, we'll turn our attention to index funds, a type of mutual fund with a specific investment strategy that aims to mirror the performance of a market index.

CHAPTER 3: INTRODUCTION TO INDEX FUNDS

In this chapter, we will explore index funds—a popular investment choice that offers broad market exposure, low operating expenses, and low portfolio turnover. These features make index funds an attractive option for investors of all levels.

3.1 Definition and History of Index Funds

An index fund is a type of mutual fund or exchange-traded fund (ETF) that aims to replicate the performance of a specific financial market index. This strategy is known as passive management. Rather than trying to outperform the market, an index fund attempts to match the market's performance.

Index funds first emerged in the 1970s and have since grown in popularity due to their simplicity and cost-effectiveness. The first index fund was created by John Bogle, the founder of The Vanguard

Group, and it tracked the S&P 500 Index.

3.2 Examples of Popular Indexes

Indexes represent a specific segment of the financial market. Here are some widely recognized indexes that are often mimicked by index funds:

- S&P 500: The U.S. stock market commonly uses an index made up of the 500 largest companies. This serves as a benchmark for performance.

- Dow Jones Industrial Average (DJIA): The DJIA includes 30 large, publicly-owned companies based in the U.S.

- Nasdaq Composite: This index includes all the stocks listed on the Nasdaq stock exchange, many of which are technology companies.

- MSCI EAFE: This index represents the performance of large and mid-cap securities across developed markets in Europe, Australasia, and the Far East.

3.3 The Benefits of Investing in Index Funds

Index funds offer several distinct advantages:

- Diversification: Like mutual funds, index funds provide broad exposure to a variety of market sectors, reducing the risk associated with individual securities.

- Cost-Effectiveness: Because they're passively managed, index funds typically have lower expense ratios than actively managed funds.

- Transparency: The holdings of an index fund are a matter of public record, updated daily. This transparency means you always know what assets you own.

3.4 The Drawbacks of Investing in Index Funds

While index funds have numerous benefits, they are not without potential downsides:

- Limited Upside: Index funds aim to match market performance, not exceed it. This means they typically won't significantly outperform the market.

- Lack of Control: Investors cannot customize the holdings of an index fund. The fund simply holds whatever securities are in the index it tracks.

- Market-Cap Weighting Bias: Many index funds are market-cap weighted, meaning companies with larger market capitalizations have a bigger influence on the fund's performance. This concentration can expose the fund to additional risks.

3.5 The Mechanics of Index Funds: Tracking, Purchase, and Sale

Index funds operate by following a particular market index. The fund manager purchases securities in the index, proportional to the index's composition.

Like mutual funds, investors can purchase or sell

shares of an index fund directly from the fund (or through a broker) at the current net asset value (NAV). Some index funds are also exchange-traded funds (ETFs), meaning they can be bought and sold on an exchange at market prices throughout the trading day.

In the following chapter, we'll compare and contrast mutual funds and index funds to help you understand their similarities and differences. This knowledge will be crucial in assisting you in choosing the right investment for your financial goals.

CHAPTER 4: COMPARING MUTUAL FUNDS AND INDEX FUNDS

Mutual funds and index funds share many similarities but also possess distinct differences. Understanding these similarities and differences will empower you to make informed investment decisions based on your financial objectives, risk tolerance, and investment horizon.

4.1 Similarities Between Mutual Funds and Index Funds

Both mutual funds and index funds are collective investment schemes that pool money from many investors to invest in a portfolio of assets. Key similarities include:

- Diversification: Both fund types offer access to a wide range of securities, helping to spread risk.

- Professional Management: Both are managed by professional fund managers.

- Accessibility: Both fund types often have low minimum investment requirements, making them accessible to individual investors.

4.2 Differences Between Mutual Funds and Index Funds

While both mutual and index funds offer many benefits, they differ in their management strategy, cost, and investment goals:

- Management Strategy: Mutual funds are usually actively managed, meaning fund managers make decisions about what securities to buy or sell. Index funds, on the other hand, are passively managed and aim to mirror the performance of a specific index.

- Costs: Because index funds are passively managed, they tend to have lower expense ratios than actively managed mutual funds.

- Investment Goals: The goal of an actively managed mutual fund is to outperform the market or its benchmark. An index fund, conversely, seeks to match the performance of its benchmark index.

4.3 Performance Comparison: Active vs Passive Management

One of the main debates in investing circles is about active vs passive management. Some research suggests that over the long term, the majority of actively managed funds do not outperform their benchmark indexes after fees are considered. However, there are exceptions, and some actively managed funds consistently beat the market.

4.4 Cost Comparison: Expense Ratios and Other Costs

Expense ratios represent the cost of owning a fund, and they can significantly impact your returns over time. Because index funds are passively managed, they typically have lower expense ratios than actively managed mutual funds. Additionally, some mutual funds charge a sales commission, known as a load, either when you buy or sell the fund. Index funds do not have these charges.

In the next chapter, we'll discuss how to construct an investment strategy that aligns with your financial goals and how mutual funds and index funds can fit into that strategy. Remember, no single investment is the best choice for all situations, and a diversified portfolio often includes a mix of different investment types.

CHAPTER 5: INVESTMENT STRATEGY

An investment strategy is a plan designed to help you achieve your financial goals. Your strategy will be shaped by several factors, including your investment horizon, risk tolerance, and financial objectives. Mutual funds and index funds can play a vital role in your strategy, providing diversification and exposure to a range of assets.

5.1 Understanding Your Financial Goals

Before making any investments, it's crucial to understand your financial goals. Are you saving for retirement, a down payment on a house, or your child's education? Each goal will have a different time horizon and may require different investment approaches.

5.2 Assessing Your Risk Tolerance

Risk tolerance refers to the extent to which

an investor is comfortable with fluctuations in investment returns. Understanding your risk tolerance is crucial as it can influence the type of assets you should invest in. Mutual funds and index funds can offer a variety of risk profiles, from conservative bond funds to more aggressive equity funds.

5.3 Building a Diversified Portfolio

Diversification is a risk management strategy that involves spreading your investments across various financial instruments, industries, and other categories to avoid excessive exposure to any single asset. Both mutual funds and index funds can provide an easy way to achieve diversification in your portfolio.

5.4 Choosing Between Mutual Funds and Index Funds

Both mutual funds and index funds can have a place in your investment strategy, and the best choice depends on your individual circumstances:

- Mutual Funds could be suitable if you believe in the potential for active management to outperform the market and are willing to pay higher fees for professional management.

- Index Funds might be a better fit if you prefer a passive investment strategy, believe in the efficiency of markets, and want to keep costs as low as possible.

5.5 Regular Monitoring and Adjustments

Once your portfolio is set up, it's important to review it periodically. The performance of your investments, changes in your financial situation, or shifts in your financial goals may require adjustments to your portfolio. Regular monitoring ensures your portfolio remains aligned with your investment strategy.

In the next chapter, we will delve into practical aspects of investing in mutual funds and index funds, such as opening an account, selecting a fund, and understanding the tax implications of your investments.

CHAPTER 6: PRACTICAL ASPECTS OF INVESTING

Having equipped yourself with an understanding of the principles and strategies of investing, let's delve into the practicalities. This chapter covers how to open an investment account, select a suitable fund, understand tax implications, and effectively monitor your investments.

6.1 Opening an Investment Account

To start investing in mutual funds or index funds, you first need to open an investment account. This can be done through various financial institutions, including banks, brokerage firms, and mutual fund companies. The process typically involves providing personal identification information, choosing an account type (individual, joint, or retirement), and funding the account.

6.2 Selecting a Suitable Fund

Choosing a suitable fund requires careful consideration. Here are some factors to look at when selecting a fund:

- Investment Objective: Ensure the fund aligns with your financial goals and risk tolerance.

- Expense Ratio: Lower costs can lead to better net returns over time.

- Past Performance: While past performance is not indicative of future results, it can provide insight into how the fund has performed in different market conditions.

- Manager Tenure and Experience: In the case of actively managed funds, it might be beneficial to consider the track record and experience of the fund manager.

6.3 Understanding Tax Implications

Understanding the tax implications of investing in mutual funds and index funds is important. In many jurisdictions, any income generated from these investments, such as dividends or capital gains, may be subject to tax. Certain types of accounts, like individual retirement accounts (IRAs) in the United States, can provide tax advantages. Consulting a tax advisor can be helpful in navigating these complexities.

6.4 Investing and Reinvesting Dividends

Some mutual funds and index funds distribute dividends to their investors. You usually have the option to either receive these dividends as cash or reinvest them back into the fund by purchasing additional shares. Reinvesting dividends can contribute to the compound growth of your investment.

6.5 Monitoring Your Investments

Once you've made your investments, it's crucial to monitor them regularly. Review your investment statements, track the performance of your funds, and stay informed about relevant market developments. This doesn't mean you should react to every market fluctuation, but regular monitoring will help you make informed decisions about when adjustments to your portfolio might be necessary.

In the final chapter, we will summarize the key points covered in this book and provide you with some concluding thoughts on investing in mutual funds and index funds.

CHAPTER 7: NAVIGATING MARKET TRENDS AND CHANGES

Investing isn't a set-it-and-forget-it activity. Market trends change and evolve, and an effective investor knows how to navigate these changes. In this final chapter, we'll discuss how to stay informed about market trends, adjust your strategy as needed, and keep a long-term perspective.

7.1 Staying Informed

Staying up-to-date with financial news and market trends is important. There are numerous resources, including financial news websites, blogs, podcasts, and newsletters, that can provide valuable insights. Remember to be critical of the information you consume and make sure it comes from reputable sources.

7.2 Navigating Market Volatility

All markets experience periods of volatility. Understanding that volatility is part of the investing process can help you remain calm during turbulent times. Instead of reacting to short-term market fluctuations, focus on your long-term investment goals and strategy.

7.3 Rebalancing Your Portfolio

Over time, some of your investments may perform better than others, leading to an asset allocation that differs from your original strategy. Rebalancing involves adjusting your portfolio back to its target allocation. This process can help maintain your desired level of risk and return.

7.4 Adjusting Your Strategy as Needed

As your life changes, so might your financial goals and risk tolerance. Regularly reassess your investment strategy to ensure it continues to align with your current circumstances and future objectives. Major life events, like marriage, having children, or nearing retirement, might necessitate changes to your strategy.

7.5 Maintaining a Long-Term Perspective

Investing is a long-term endeavor. While it can be tempting to chase after the latest hot stock or jump on the bandwagon during a market rally, a disciplined, long-term approach often leads to more consistent results. Mutual funds and index funds, with their diversification benefits and ease of management, can be effective tools for long-term investors.

In conclusion, investing in mutual funds and index funds can be a powerful way to grow your wealth and achieve your financial goals. By understanding how these funds work, choosing investments that align with your objectives, and maintaining a disciplined investment strategy, you can navigate the ups and downs of the market and move closer to financial success.

CONCLUSION: BECOMING A SAVVY INVESTOR

We have embarked on a journey together through the world of mutual funds and index funds, uncovering the complexities and opportunities these investment vehicles offer. This journey, like any in the realm of personal finance, is an ongoing one. As your understanding deepens, you'll find yourself better equipped to navigate the financial markets and make decisions that align with your goals.

Remember, investing is not about short-term wins, but building long-term wealth. Mutual funds and index funds are tools designed for this very purpose. They offer diversification, professional management, and a means to participate in a wide range of market segments. With these tools in your arsenal, you are well on your way to becoming a savvy investor.

Yet, the most successful investors are not just those who understand their investments, but those who understand themselves. Your financial goals, risk tolerance, and investment horizon are all crucial components of your investment strategy. Align your investments with these personal factors, and you're likely to find the journey far more rewarding.

In the dynamic world of investing, change is the only constant. Keeping informed about market trends and adjusting your strategy when needed will help you stay on track. Patience and discipline are your allies on this journey.

Embrace the learning process. Mistakes may happen, but they offer valuable lessons. Consult trusted financial advisors when needed, and never stop expanding your knowledge.

In the end, the journey to financial prosperity is a personal one. While the path may be fraught with complexity and change, it also brings opportunity. By equipping yourself with knowledge, maintaining a long-term perspective, and staying committed to your financial goals, you're not just investing in the market—you're investing in yourself.

Here's to your financial future, and your continuing journey as a savvy investor.

APPENDIX: INVESTMENT GLOSSARY

Below you'll find definitions for some common investment terms that you might come across in your investing journey.

Active Management: This is a strategy wherein expert fund managers invest in specific stocks or assets with the aim of surpassing the investment benchmark index.

Asset Allocation: The strategy of dividing investments among different asset classes, such as stocks, bonds, and cash, to optimize the risk/reward tradeoff based on an individual's specific situation and goals.

Benchmark: A standard against which the performance of a security, mutual fund, or investment manager can be measured. For example, the S&P 500 is often used as a benchmark for equity funds.

Bond: A bond is a type of investment where an investor loans money to a borrower, typically a corporation or government. Bondholders receive regular interest payments and are paid back the original amount of the loan when it matures.

Capital Gain: When the value of an investment or asset goes up and becomes worth more than its original purchase price, it is known as capital appreciation.

Diversification: A strategy for managing risk that involves diversifying investments across a portfolio with a wide range of options.

Dividend: A payment made by a corporation to its shareholders, usually in the form of cash or additional shares.

Equity: Ownership interest in a corporation in the form of common or preferred stock.

Exchange-Traded Fund (ETF): ETFs are a type of investment fund that can be traded on stock exchanges, just like stocks. Although they resemble mutual funds, they can be bought and sold like stocks.

Expense Ratio: A measure of what it costs an investment company to operate a mutual fund, expressed as a percentage of the fund's average net assets.

Index: A statistical indicator providing a representation of the value of the securities which constitute it. Indices often serve as benchmarks for measuring investment performance— for example, the Dow Jones Industrial Average or the S&P 500.

Mutual Fund: An investment vehicle made up of a pool of funds collected from many investors for the purpose of investing in securities such as stocks, bonds, money market instruments, and other assets.

Passive Management: An investing strategy that aims to mirror the performance of a benchmark index. It's the opposite of active management.

Portfolio: This is a portfolio of financial investments that include stocks, bonds, commodities, cash, and cash equivalents, as well as mutual funds and ETFs.

Rebalancing: The process of realigning the weightings of a portfolio of assets to maintain a desired asset allocation.

Risk Tolerance: An investor's ability or willingness to endure declines in the prices of investments.

Stock: This refers to a security that demonstrates ownership in a corporation and denotes a right to a portion of the corporation's assets and earnings.

Volatility: Volatility is a statistical measure of how much a security or market index's returns vary.

Generally, a higher level of volatility means that the security is riskier.

BIBLIOGRAPHY AND REFERENCES

1. Bogle, John C. (1999). *Common Sense on Mutual Funds: New Imperatives for the Intelligent Investor*. John Wiley & Sons.

2. Malkiel, Burton G. (2003). *A Random Walk Down Wall Street: The Time-Tested Strategy for Successful Investing*. W. W. Norton & Company.

3. Ferri, Richard A. (2007). *The ETF Book: All You Need to Know About Exchange-Traded Funds*. Wiley.

4. Swedroe, Larry E. (2011). *The Only Guide to a Winning Investment Strategy You'll Ever Need: The Way Smart Money Invests Today*. St. Martin's Griffin.

5. Swensen, David F. (2009). *Pioneering Portfolio Management: An Unconventional Approach to Institutional Investment*. Free Press.

6. "Mutual Funds and ETFs: A Guide for Investors". U.S. Securities and Exchange Commission. https://

www.sec.gov/reportspubs/investor-publications/investorpubsinwsmfhtm.html

7. "Investing in Index Funds". U.S. News & World Report. https://money.usnews.com/investing/investing-101/articles/what-is-an-index-fund

8. "How to Pick a Mutual Fund". Morningstar. https://www.morningstar.com/articles/957487/how-to-pick-a-mutual-fund

9. "Mutual Funds vs. Index Funds: Which Should You Choose in 2022?". NerdWallet. https://www.nerdwallet.com/article/investing/mutual-fund-vs-index-fund-the-difference

10. "Mutual Funds and Taxes". Fidelity Investments. https://www.fidelity.com/learning-center/personal-finance/tax-savings-strategies/mutual-funds-taxes

DISCLAIMER

Disclaimer: The author of this book is not a licensed financial professional and the information contained within is not intended to be taken as financial advice. Investing in stocks and other securities carries a risk of loss. Please consult a licensed financial advisor and conduct your own research before making any investment decisions.

It is also important to consult with a tax professional when dealing with tax implications of investing, especially when it comes to reporting, as tax laws and rules may vary depending on the country or state and the circumstances.

www.ingramcontent.com/pod-product-compliance
Ingram Content Group UK Ltd.
Pitfield, Milton Keynes, MK11 3LW, UK
UKHW021538100325
4931UKWH00035B/210